Destroying Trump

The Left's Obsession to Take Down the President and What It Means for America

MARK PANTANO

Table of Contents

Introduction

Every four or eight years, as we inaugurate a new President of the United States, we acknowledge how truly unique and special our country is. We celebrate the peaceful transition of power from one administration to the next, which has proceeded unbroken since George Washington took the Oath of Office in 1789. Well, no longer. While this quintessentially American tradition has thus far continued, it is no longer respected by a significant number of Americans. The modern American Left, which now has complete control of the Democrat Party, no longer even pretends to honor our country's history and traditions, or to respect the constitutional processes of our republic. The election of Donald Trump has laid bare the anti-Americanism and hatred that lies at the heart of the Left and today's Democrat Party.

The Left has decided that it no longer believes in democratic elections or in governing ourselves in accordance with the processes prescribed by the Constitution. What the Left wants is mob rule – they being the mob, of course. They are to have their way, whether they win elections or not. When they do win elections, they are happy to pretend to believe in constitutional government. When they lose however, they drop the pretense. They demonstrate, for all to see, their disdain for our system. It is a sickness. A sickness which stems from self-importance, a perverted sense of entitlement, and a dream of a

Leftist Utopia which cannot exist and the pursuit of which leads only to authoritarianism, misery, and death. It is a sickness of hatred masquerading as compassion. A sickness of arrogant self-righteousness which leads them to reject the system of law and tradition that undergirds our civil society, in order to achieve their immediate political demands.

A manifestation of this sickness is the Left's open rejection of the results of the 2016 Presidential Election. The problem is not simply that they are shocked and angered over the election of President Trump, it is that they refuse to accept his legitimacy. Leaders within the Democrat Party encouraged their followers to reject Trump as President. At the time of Trump's Inauguration, they encouraged use of the slogan "Not My President" and organized protests with that phrase as their rallying cry.[1] They self-identify as part of "The Resistance," as if they are rebel fighters trying to overthrow a despotic emperor

---

[1] Kate Abbey-Lambertz, Hayley Miller, and Kim Bellware, "Thousands Rally At Anti-Trump 'Not My Presidents Day' Events," *Huffington Post*, February 20, 2017, https://www.huffingtonpost.com/entry/not-my-presidents-day-protests_us_58ab1f9ce4b07602ad56cece.

Shira Tarlo, "'Not My President's Day': Thousands Protest at Anti-Trump Rallies Across U.S.," *NBC News*, February 20, 2017, https://www.nbcnews.com/politics/donald-trump/not-my-president-s-day-thousands-plan-anti-trump-rallies-n722586.

Eric Levenson, "'Not My President's Day' protesters rally to oppose Trump," *CNN*, February 21, 2017, http://www.cnn.com/2017/02/20/us/not-my-presidents-day-protests/index.html.

who has claimed their lands.[2] Even their defeated presidential candidate, Hillary Clinton, announced that she herself was part of The Resistance.[3] This is sick. This is profoundly un-American. This is dangerous.

Whatever your thoughts about President Trump, they are irrelevant to this issue. I will offer no defense or promotion of Donald Trump or his policy positions in these pages. I will not even discuss his positions, actions, or statements. This is not about Donald Trump. This is about the subversion of the principles upon which our republic was founded. This is about tearing down the system, which has allowed a diverse people of differing political opinions and ways of life to exist as a prosperous nation, in order to benefit the short-term political fortunes of one political party and to feed the hateful passions of its supporters. This is about putting the future of our country at great risk. In short, this is about the sickness of the American Left and the damage they are doing to the country.

---

[2] Joshua Holland, "Your Guide to the Sprawling New Anti-Trump Resistance Movement," *The Nation*, February 6, 2017, https://www.thenation.com/article/your-guide-to-the-sprawling-new-anti-trump-resistance-movement/.

[3] Alexander Burns, "Clinton, Denouncing Trump, Calls Herself 'Part of the Resistance,'" *The New York Times*, May 2, 2017, https://www.nytimes.com/2017/05/02/us/clinton-trump-interview.html?mtrref=www.google.com.

It is from this perspective that we must evaluate the tactics of the Left as they seek to destroy the Trump Presidency. This book is not about Donald Trump per se. It is about our country. It is about the peaceful continuity of our republic, and the grave threat posed to it by the un-American tactics of the Left and the Democrat Party

Election Hysteria

The American Left, including the Democrat Party, their assortment of affiliated hate-groups, and nearly all of the Establishment Media, has been in a state of open hysteria since Donald Trump was elected President on November 8, 2016. As I write these words, it is early May 2017, and the hysteria has not subsided at all. To the contrary, in many ways it has intensified and begun to take on the contours of a serious problem. The Left has begun to organize this hysteria and focus it into strategy. Having now realized that emotional breakdowns and meaningless protest marches are not going to force a constitutionally-elected President from office, the Democrat Left is devising political strategies aimed at taking him down.

The Left's efforts to force President Trump from office are, at this point at least, still chaotic. They have not settled on a clear strategy. They are throwing everything at the wall in the hope that something sticks. Their strategy follows the news cycle. Anything and everything that Trump says or does is cause for the latest faux-outrage. Every statement that he makes, every action that he takes, is said to be "a threat to democracy," "a step towards dictatorship," or "a constitutional crisis."

Of course, these hysterical assertions are ridiculous – and the leaders of the Left, including elected Democrats, know that they are ridiculous. However, they also know that about one-third of the country, their political base, is made up of certified crazy people who will believe all of it. They intentionally keep these people on the verge of insanity, blinded by hatred and an irrational fear of President Trump. In this state of constant panic and hysterical overreaction, these followers will do whatever they are told or encouraged to do by their leaders.

Acting in unison, like the good little drones that they are, they will protest, march, riot, intimidate, harass and assault. They will crash town hall meetings of Republican Congressmen and make spectacles of themselves for the TV cameras.[4] Taking time away from their "Gender Studies" and "White Privilege" classes, they will burn cars, trash local businesses, and damage property when a pro-Trump author attempts to

---

[4] Mark Z. Barabak and John Cherwa, "Loud and angry, protesters turn congressional town halls into must-see political TV," *The Los Angeles Times*, February 22, 2017, http://www.latimes.com/politics/la-na-pol-townhalls-voter-mood-20170222-story.html.

speak on a college campus.[5] They will pepper spray young female Trump supporters in the face,[6] while accusing President Trump of hating women. They will commit aggravated assault by hitting people at Trump rallies with pipes and metal bike locks,[7] while denouncing President Trump as a violent fascist. And, of course, they will send money to the Democrat Party!

By keeping their followers constantly agitated, and by encouraging hysteria and anarchy, they hope to influence the rest of the country. They want to convince as many people as possible that the country is falling apart, and that it is specifically because Donald Trump is President. They believe that if they can instill a fear and hatred of Trump in enough people, then those people will support any method of removing him from office.

---

[5] James Doubek, "Breitbart Editor's Event Canceled As Protests Turn Violent At UC Berkeley," National Public Radio, February 2, 2017, https://www.npr.org/sections/thetwo-way/2017/02/02/512992000/breitbart-editors-event-canceled-as-protests-turn-violent-at-uc-berkeley.

[6] Dave Urbanski, "VIDEO: Female Trump Supporter Pepper-Sprayed at U.C. Berkeley Riot — But Not by Police," *The Blaze*, February 2, 2017, http://www.theblaze.com/news/2017/02/02/video-female-trump-supporter-pepper-sprayed-at-u-c-berkeley-riot-but-not-by-police.

[7] Brittany M. Hughes, "Shocking Video Shows Antifa Rioters Beating a Trump Supporter With a Bike Lock," *MRCTV.org*, April 20, 2017, https://www.mrctv.org/blog/shocking-video-shows-antifa-rioters-beating-trump-supporter-bike-lock.

Driving or removing President Trump from office is all that matters to the Left. They discuss little else. You would struggle in vain to find a single elected Democrat anywhere in Washington, D.C. who is discussing or proposing anything related to public policy. Every waking moment of their political lives is devoted to taking down the President – and any method will do. Whether he resigns, is impeached and removed, is incapacitated, or is forcefully overthrown by a banana republic-style military coup, they don't much care. Getting Trump out is all that matters. They are obsessed.

PART I Removing President Trump from Office

We know they despise him, but what can the Left actually do to remove President Trump from office? As I stated, Leftists do not care how he is removed – only that he is. Given the perverted nature of their group psychology, and their infinite capacity for hatred, Leftists would be ecstatic if Trump were removed even by illegal or violent means. I will not lend credibility to any illegitimate means of removing a President by discussing them here. Rather, I will briefly discuss the legal methods by which a President can be removed from office, as prescribed by the Constitution.

There are three legal methods by which a President of the United States can be effectively removed from the powers of his office. The first, and most obvious way, is by resignation. The second is for him to be declared unable to discharge the duties of the Presidency. While this method does not technically remove him from office, it does strip him of his constitutional authority. The third is for Congress to remove him. This method requires impeachment in the House of Representatives and conviction in the Senate.

Resignation

A President may resign. This is the simplest way for Trump to leave office before his term expires. Period. End of story. No mystery here. The Constitution references a President's resignation as follows:

Article 2, Section 1, Clause 6

*In case of the removal of the President from office, or of his death, **resignation**, or inability to discharge the powers and duties of the said office, the same shall devolve on the Vice President, and the Congress may by law provide for the case of removal, death, resignation or inability, both of the President and Vice President, declaring what officer shall then act as President, and such officer shall act accordingly, until the disability be removed, or a President shall be elected.*

(emphasis added)

25th Amendment, Section 1

*In case of the removal of the President from office or of his death or **resignation**, the Vice President shall become President.*

(emphasis added)

The question with respect to President Trump resigning is not whether or not it is possible, the question is one of likelihood. Pondering this question requires a discussion of politics.

The Politics of Resignation

Broadly speaking, there are two main reasons a President would resign from office. The first would be that he wants to, for whatever reason. The second is that he is politically forced to choose resignation as the best of his available options given whatever circumstances exist at the time.

Voluntary Resignation

Not knowing President Trump personally, I have no idea what, if anything, would motivate him to want to resign. Therefore, I have no way to analyze the likelihood of this ever happening. What I do know however, is that convincing Trump to want to resign is an obvious objective of the Left and the Democrat Party. Their strategy is clear in this regard. They want to make Trump so miserable being President that he decides he no longer wants to do it.

Leftists hope that Trump can be persuaded to resign because of who they believe he is. They view him as a rich and famous person whose only true goal in life is to be rich and famous. They believe that his run for the Presidency had little to do with any real interest in politics or governing, but rather was a stunt to feed his ego and satiate his lust for publicity and adoration.[8] In fact, according to some, he never expected, or even necessarily wanted, to win. His whole candidacy was some sort of joke that took on a life of its own. Once he discovered that winning the Presidency was an actual possibility, only then did he become serious about wanting to be President. Even then, and to this day, Trump is not really interested in the duties and responsibilities of the Presidency, his only interest is in being President. This is what the Left believes. Whether they are correct, or not, is irrelevant to their strategy. All that matters is that they believe it to be true.

Given this view of Trump, the Democrats believe that if they can make being President sufficiently unpleasant, then he will simply quit. After all, since his decision to run for President was made on a whim, so too could his decision to quit be made flippantly.

As their theory goes, Trump loves being loved. If they can manufacture enough hatred of the President, he will just walk away. Eventually he will decide that he would rather go back to his old life of being a jet-setting billionaire without a care in the world. He's been President, fine. He can check that off his list and use it to stroke his ego. But why put up with the hassle and stress? Just walk away and go be rich! That is what

---

[8] Maggie Haberman and Alexander Burns, "Donald Trump's Presidential Run Began in an Effort to Gain Stature," *The New York Times*, March 12, 2016, https://www.nytimes.com/2016/03/13/us/politics/donald-trump-campaign.html?mtrref=www.google.com.

the Left is hoping for. Will it happen? I have no way of knowing, though I rather doubt it. Either way, it is a possibility, so they will pursue it.

Forced Resignation

If they cannot make President Trump want to resign, then perhaps they can force him to resign. This method of getting Trump to resign is similar to the one just described, but with an important difference. Under this scenario, President Trump would resign, not necessarily because the experience of being President is a miserable one, but as a calculated step to avoid some specific negative consequence.

The ways in which such a scenario could unfold are limitless. It would depend upon the factual circumstances and, more than likely, the degree of popular opposition to the President at the time. Some type of scandal or potential criminal wrongdoing is the most likely vehicle for pursing this strategy. To this end, the Left is doing everything they can to uncover (or manufacture) anything that President Trump has said or done that has the slightest whiff of scandal. We have already been witness to all sorts of allegations, many seemingly made up out of whole cloth. Who knows what we will hear in the months and years ahead. One thing is certain, the allegations, baseless or not, will be never-ending as long as Donald Trump is President.

The Left's goal is to find some incident, action, statement, or allegation which can be used to apply enough political pressure to President Trump that he is forced to resign. That is why almost everything he does is labelled as an "impeachable offense," a "constitutional crisis," "something a fascist dictator would do," or whatever hyperbolic terminology their obsessive little minds can conjure up. Thus far, none of these supposedly scandalous actions have generated the type of outrage that would lead to impeachment proceedings or cause the public to turn against him en masse. But, no matter, the Leftist hordes are just getting warmed-up. As long as Trump is President, the witch hunt will continue.

If the Leftists ever find, or manufacture, an issue that is perceived to be serious enough, they hope to use it as leverage to force his resignation. Under this scenario, Trump would resign in order to avoid impeachment proceedings, public humiliation or condemnation, anguish of his family, or some other negative consequence that could befall him by remaining in office.

In most scenarios which can be constructed in one's mind as to how this would unfold, the key to success of this strategy lies in public opinion. It is hard to imagine a President being forced to resign unless public opinion turns overwhelmingly against him. An exception would be if the public did not yet know the whole story and the President resigns in hopes of preventing its revelation.

13

Given what we know of Donald Trump, and what he has already endured in public, it is hard to imagine him resigning just to avoid embarrassment. For Trump to resign, there would likely need to be a greater potential consequence to his remaining in office.

Another important consideration is the Republican Party. If President Trump were forced to resign, pressure to do so by his own party would almost certainly be involved. This is not to suggest that Trump would resign just because prominent members of the GOP want him to – far from it. While President Trump is a Republican, he is hardly a party man.

While running for office, candidate Trump was vehemently opposed by the vast majority of the Republican Establishment. Once he was elected, most fell in line behind him, if only for appearance. But make no mistake, Trump is still disliked by most of the Establishment and, though they do not state so publicly, they would love to see him gone. That being said, as long as Trump retains the support of Republican voters, the Establishment is unlikely to join any effort by the Left to force him out. However, if Republican voters ever turn against the President in large numbers, or if credible evidence of actual and serious wrongdoing by Trump were uncovered, then Republicans would join with Democrats and the Left in less time than it takes Barack Obama to praise himself.

Inability to Discharge Presidential Duties: The 25th Amendment

There is another way to effectively remove Donald Trump from power – the 25th Amendment. This constitutional provision establishes a process of presidential succession. Importantly, for purposes of this discussion, it addresses a potential situation in which a President is "unable to discharge the powers and duties of his office." While a President cannot be removed from office pursuant to this amendment, he can be completely stripped of his authority.

The 25th Amendment reads as follows:

Section 1
In case of the removal of the President from office or of his death or resignation, the Vice President shall become President.

Section 2
Whenever there is a vacancy in the office of the Vice President, the President shall nominate a Vice President who shall take office upon confirmation by a majority vote of both Houses of Congress.

Section 3

Whenever the President transmits to the President pro tempore of the Senate and the Speaker of the House of Representatives his written declaration that he is unable to discharge the powers and duties of his office, and until he transmits to them a written declaration to the contrary, such powers and duties shall be discharged by the Vice President as Acting President.

Section 4

Whenever the Vice President and a majority of either the principal officers of the executive departments or of such other body as Congress may by law provide, transmit to the President pro tempore of the Senate and the Speaker of the House of Representatives their written declaration that the President is unable to discharge the powers and duties of his office, the Vice President shall immediately assume the powers and duties of the office as Acting President.

Thereafter, when the President transmits to the President pro tempore of the Senate and the Speaker of the House of Representatives his written declaration that no inability exists, he shall resume the powers and duties of his office unless the Vice President and a majority of either the principal officers of the executive department or of such other body as Congress may by law provide, transmit within four days to the President pro tempore of the Senate and the Speaker of the House of Representatives their written declaration that the President is unable to discharge the powers and duties of his office. Thereupon Congress shall decide the issue, assembling within forty-eight hours for that purpose if not in session. If the Congress, within twenty-one days after receipt of the latter written declaration, or, if Congress is not in session, within twenty-one days after Congress is required to assemble, determines by two-thirds vote of both Houses that the President is unable to discharge the powers and duties of his office, the Vice President shall continue to discharge the same as Acting President; otherwise, the President shall resume the powers and duties of his office.

Sections 3 and 4 establish a process whereby a President may either voluntarily relinquish, or be involuntarily relieved of his authority. Under either scenario, the underlying reason for doing so must be that the President is "unable to discharge the powers and duties of his office." The amendment requires no particular factual circumstances which would justify taking such action, but what is most obviously envisioned is some type of mental or physical disability. That being said however, any circumstances which cause the President to be unable to function in office would justify invoking these sections.

Section 3 provides that the President, based on his own determination, may voluntarily relinquish his authority. He would do so by transmitting "to the President pro tempore of the Senate and the Speaker of the House of Representatives his written declaration that he is unable to discharge the powers and duties of his office." Upon such transmittal, the Vice President shall immediately assume the powers and duties as "Acting President." The President may reclaim his authority by transmitting another written declaration to the President pro tempore of the Senate and the Speaker of the House of Representatives, in which he advises that he is no longer unable to discharge the powers and duties of his office. Under this section, a President's surrender of his authority may be temporary, or, if the disabling circumstances persist, it may last for the duration of his term.

For purposes of the Left's effort to remove President Trump from office or to strip him of his constitutional authority, Section 3 is not particularly useful as it requires the President to relinquish power voluntarily. However, that is not the case under Section 4, which could be used to strip the President of his power against his will.

Under Section 4, the Vice President and a majority of either the President's Cabinet or another body which may be established by Congress, can strip the President of his authority if they determine that he is "unable to discharge the powers and duties of his office." They do so, as the President himself would do under Section 3, by transmitting "to the President pro tempore of the Senate and the Speaker of the House of Representatives their written declaration that the President is unable to discharge the powers and duties of his office." Upon such transmittal, the Vice President shall immediately assume the powers and duties as "Acting President."

After being stripped of his authority under Section 4, the President may reclaim his authority by transmitting his own declaration to Congress advising that no inability exists. Upon such transmittal, the President shall resume the powers of his office unless the Vice President and a majority of either the President's Cabinet or another body which may be established by Congress, transmit to Congress within four days another declaration reaffirming that the President is "unable to discharge the powers and duties of his office." After that, the issue will be decided by Congress itself. If Congress votes by a two-thirds majority in both Houses that the President is "unable to discharge the powers and duties of his office," then the Vice President shall continue serving as "Acting President."

The confusing back-and-forth nature of this process aside, Section 4 does provide a way for the President to be stripped of his authority against his will. Of course, to do so would be very difficult as it would ultimately require the collaboration of the Vice President, a majority of either the

President's Cabinet or another body which may be established by Congress, and two-thirds of both Houses of Congress.

While it may seem ludicrous to think that Democrats and the Left would seriously attempt to have President Trump involuntarily stripped of his authority under Section 4 of the 25th Amendment, I caution you not to dismiss this possibility so quickly. As I have stated, the Left is trying to destroy Trump and his presidency by any means necessary. Well, this is a means by which they can, so expect them to try.

In fact, there have already been signs of Leftists laying the groundwork for just such an attempt. You have likely observed them yourself. Every time you hear someone suggest that Trump is "unfit for office," you should be thinking about the 25th Amendment. Since before he took office, there have been Leftists in the Democrat Party, in the media, in academia, and elsewhere insisting that Trump's behavior, in one way or another, is evidence of mental illness. Why do you think they would be making such statements? Certainly, most average know-nothing Leftists speak this way because they themselves are insane or demented by hate. However, this does not explain all such talk. Many leaders of the Left, particularly elected Democrats, make these types of statements precisely with Section 4 of the 25th Amendment in mind.

Removing a President: Impeachment and Conviction

The only way for a President to be removed from office before expiration of his term, without him doing so himself by resignation, is through Congress. The process requires impeachment in the House of Representatives and conviction in the Senate. To date, no President of the United States has ever been removed from office in this way. Two Presidents, Andrew Johnson and Bill Clinton, were impeached by the House but not convicted in the Senate.

The sections of the Constitution relevant to impeachment and removal of the President are as follows:

Article 2, Section 4
The President, Vice President and all civil officers of the United States, shall be removed from office on impeachment for, and conviction of, treason, bribery, or other high crimes and misdemeanors.

25th Amendment, Section 1
In case of the removal of the President from office or of his death or resignation, the Vice President shall become President.

Article 1, Section 2, Clause 5
The House of Representatives shall choose their speaker
and other officers; and shall have the sole power of
impeachment.

Article 1, Section 3, Clause 6
The Senate shall have the sole power to try all
impeachments. When sitting for that purpose, they shall
be on oath or affirmation. When the President of the
United States is tried, the Chief Justice shall preside: And
no person shall be convicted without the concurrence of two
thirds of the members present.

The Process of Removing a President

Article II of the Constitution establishes the Executive Branch of the federal government – The President – and describes the scope of his authority, duties, and obligations. Section 4 of Article II provides for the removal of the President by a two-step process: impeachment, followed by conviction. He may be removed from office for "treason, bribery, or other high crimes and misdemeanors."

Article I of the Constitution establishes the Legislative Branch of the federal government – Congress – and describes the scope of its authority, duties and obligations. Section 2, Clause 5 of Article I grants "the sole power of impeachment" to the House of Representatives. Therefore, any effort to remove the President must begin in the House. Charges of "treason, bribery, or other high crimes and misdemeanors" are filed in the House as "articles of impeachment." If, by majority vote, the House approves one or more articles of impeachment, then the President is impeached. Any articles of impeachment which are approved by the House will be sent to the Senate which, pursuant to Section 3, Clause 6 of Article I, has "the sole power to try all impeachments." A two-thirds majority vote in the Senate is required to convict the President. If the President is convicted on one or more articles of impeachment, then he shall be removed from office. The 25th Amendment provides that when a President is removed from office, the Vice President shall become President.

The Politics of Impeachment

"Impeachment," which is often used as a shorthand expression for the constitutional process of removing a President (as explained above), is a political remedy. It is important to understand that, while allegations of criminality may form the basis of articles of impeachment, the impeachment process itself is not a criminal or legal matter.

First, criminal allegations are not necessarily required to impeach a President. Article 2, Section 4 defines impeachable offenses for which a President may be removed from office as "treason, bribery, or other high crimes and misdemeanors."

While treason and bribery are specific crimes, the phrase "high crimes and misdemeanors" is ambiguous and open to interpretation. While the exact meaning of this phrase is the subject of debate among constitutional scholars, it is widely-agreed to include actions which would not necessarily constitute violations of criminal law. Discussions of this issue among the Framers during the Constitutional Convention, make clear that the intent behind the impeachment process was to allow Congress to remove a President who has engaged in some type of serious misconduct which, by its nature, is injurious to the public or which constitutes a dereliction of duty, but which may not amount to criminal violations. For example, while not necessarily criminal, a President's willful violation of the Constitution, by taking an action which knowingly exceeds his authority, would certainly be grounds for impeachment. Impeachment is not for the purpose of punishment, but rather a remedial action to protect the country from harmful actions of the President. Therefore, impeachment is inherently a political question.

Second, even if articles of impeachment allege criminal violations, the process itself falls far outside the criminal justice system. Most notably, it is held in Congress, not in the courts, where criminal trials and other legal matters are litigated. Charges (articles of impeachment) are approved, not by a grand jury as in criminal cases, but by a majority vote of politicians. There are no rules of evidence or criminal procedure which, in the legal system, are designed to ensure that only the most reliable evidence is considered and that the constitutional rights of the accused are protected. Unlike criminal trials, where a defendant is convicted only if his guilt is proven "beyond a reasonable doubt," there is no standard of proof required to impeach or remove a President. Similarly, while those who harbor prejudices, which could impact their objectivity, are prevented from serving on juries in criminal and civil cases, Congressmen and Senators can cast their votes based on their political biases alone if they wish.

Finally, the impeachment and conviction of a President is a non-justiciable issue. In other words, a President who is removed from office cannot appeal his impeachment or conviction to the courts. The Constitution grants sole authority over the removal of a President to Congress alone. It is a political issue to be handled by the elected representatives of the People, not a legal matter subject to adjudication by the courts.

The Legitimacy of Impeachment

If Donald Trump, or any other President, commits "treason, bribery, or other high crimes and misdemeanors" by engaging in misconduct which is injurious to the public or to the proper discharge of the duties and obligations of the Presidency, then he should rightly be impeached and removed from office. However, for Congress to seek the removal of a constitutionally-elected President in this way, it had better do so for good cause and with a process, and its end result, that is viewed by a substantial majority of the country as just and fair. To do otherwise would have the potential of causing more harm to the country than whatever wrong was ostensibly remedied by his removal. Removal of a President by Congress was intended to be a last resort. It should not be considered lightly, or for purely partisan political reasons.

Unfortunately, what the Left is attempting to do, is treat the impeachment process as if it were just another political tactic – on par with lying to voters or reporting fraudulent public polling results. Having become so obsessed with hated for President Trump, they believe it is a moral imperative to remove him from office by any means necessary. If it takes impeaching Trump for some fabricated allegation of misconduct, then so be it. If they can find something which actually is improper, no matter how insignificant or unserious, which they can distort and exaggerate beyond all reasonable proportions, all the better. The facts matter not. The law matters not. The county matters not. All that matters is destroying Trump as thoroughly and as quickly as possible. Consequences be damned! That is why almost every action taken by Trump thus far has been reacted to with calls for impeachment. Everything he does is viewed by the Left in the light most unfavorable, and most ridiculous. Everything is argued to be the action of a "dictator." Everything is an "abuse of power." The Left has already decided that President Trump should be impeached and removed from office, all that remains is to find a justification.

The 2018 Elections

The ultimate fate of the Donald Trump Presidency may be decided by the 2018 midterm elections. It is impossible to predict at this early date, by any method other than guessing, how the elections will turn out. Eighteen months is a lifetime in politics, and events, which cannot be anticipated, may greatly influence the vote.

If Democrats win control of the House of Representatives, an outcome that is not hard to imagine, it is a virtual certainty that they will attempt to impeach President Trump when they take power in 2019. Not only have they been calling for Trump's impeachment since before he took office, but I expect that many Democrats will make impeachment a central issue of their 2018 campaigns. If so, not only would Trump's impeachment be demanded by Democrat voters, it will have been promised to them. Considering the level of anti-Trump hysteria that they have cultivated in their supporters, if Democrats do win the House, they would face a political mutiny if they do not try to impeach him.

Thus, if Democrats do take control of the House of Representatives, the chances are good that President Trump will be impeached, since only a simple majority vote is required. Also, as previously discussed, impeachment is a political process, not a legal one. Evidence of a crime is not necessary, let alone the degree of proof required to convict a person in a court of law. In truth, the House can impeach the President for anything they assert constitutes a "high crime" or "misdemeanor." Given their penchant for hyperbole, they will have little trouble generating a laundry list of impeachable offenses.

If impeached, Trump's ultimate political fate will be decided by the Senate. At that point, the Democrats will face a very steep uphill battle. First of all, unless 2018 proves to be a wave election for Democrats across the country, there is little chance that they will take control of the Senate. Second, convicting a President in the Senate requires a two-thirds majority vote. Absent very serious allegations of wrongdoing, along with substantial evidence, it is hard to imagine the Senate voting to convict.

Whether President Trump is impeached and removed from office or not, if Democrats win control of the House in 2018, America will almost certainly be consumed by the politics of impeachment in 2019 and, perhaps, into 2020. Given the depth and intensity of the current political divisions in our country, this would have the potential for disaster.

PART II Leftist Hate and the Road Ahead

What will become of the Trump Presidency? Will he be a fabulously successful two-term President? Will he resign? Will he leave Washington in shame after being impeached and removed from office? Will he be stripped of his authority under the 25th Amendment? I do not know. I cannot predict the future.

What I do know with 100 percent certainty, is that as long as Donald Trump is President, the whole of the American Left will do everything they possibly can to remove him from office, or have him stripped of his power, by whatever means necessary. So consumed are they by hatred for Donald Trump that there are literally no lengths to which they would not go, and no depths to which they would not sink, in order to destroy him. If you do not recognize this, then you do not understand what the Democrats and the Left have become.

The modern American Left, whose political vehicle is the Democrat Party, is a disparate collection of interest groups. Each group is defined by whatever particular issue, or set of issues, about which they purport to be most concerned. They are not held together under one political party by fidelity to a common set of principles, for they have no principles – unless envy, bitterness, and hatred can be considered principles. For the most part, their beliefs are nothing more than a contradictory set of demands.

What binds the Left together, more than anything else, is hatred. Hatred for the American culture. Hatred for our history. Hatred for our constitutional system which limits the power of government in order to maximize the freedom of the individual. In many ways, hatred for America itself. And importantly, hatred for anyone who stands against them as they seek to destroy the objects of their contempt.

During the eight years of the Obama Presidency, this hate intensified, grew, and spread. Led by a man who never missed an opportunity to verbally trash his own country and its history, the Democrat Party left all pretenses of being reasonable or moderate behind and turned hard-left. The extreme Left is now the base of the Democrat Party. Hatred now controls.

While this hatred for America and her institutions grew exponentially during the Obama Presidency, encouraged in many ways by Obama himself, it had no outlet. After all, their Leftist Savior was President! But hatred cannot be contained for long, it must find expression. With the election of Donald Trump, the Left finally had the excuse to give expression to their hate. Trump would be cast as the personification of everything the Left despises.

The hate exploded into rage on November 8, 2016 – the day Trump was elected President of the United States. What made it incalculably worse than it might otherwise have been is the fact that the Left did not see it coming. They were convinced that Hillary Clinton would win. Due to the fraudulent media coverage of the election, and manipulated polling data, they did not even seriously consider the possibility that Donald Trump might actually be victorious. Therefore, when he did win, it was more than just a disappointment – it was like a violent shock to their system. So surprising was Trump's victory to the Left, that they could only process it emotionally (which, of course, is the only way they can process most things). They had so convinced themselves that Trump would lose, that they could not make rational sense of his victory. Therefore, instead of just the disappointment which normally follows an election loss, what came to the surface was their hatred. Pure, unfiltered hatred. This has caused the Left to react in ways that are not normal or healthy for a republic.

Rather than accepting the results of the election, they have convinced themselves that the election itself was illegitimate. Primarily, they argue that the process which had elected President Trump was corrupt. Immediately, Leftists attacked the Constitution and the Electoral College.[9] They even attempted to persuade Trump electors to switch their

---

[9] Igor Bobic, "Democrats Push For Electoral College Reform After Hillary Clinton's Popular Vote Victory," *Huffington Post*, December 6, 2016, https://www.huffingtonpost.com/entry/electoral-college-popular-vote-reform_us_58471c4be4b0ebac58070c85.

votes and install Hillary Clinton as President.[10] Next, and ever since, they began to convince themselves of some version of a nebulous conspiracy that was responsible for stealing the election from Clinton and handing it to Trump. Ultimately however, whatever story they tell themselves, at its heart is the idea that Donald Trump is not a legitimate President. [11]

Having convinced themselves that Trump seized control of the Presidency through unjust means, they feel justified in wresting power away from him by whatever means necessary. This is now the Left's obsession. They are not interested in opposing Trump politically, they seek to destroy him personally. As long as Donald Trump remains President, this will be their primary focus.

What to Expect

It is clear that the Left wants to destroy President Trump and overturn the results of the 2016 election by driving

---

[10] David S. Cohen, "Will Electors Vote Their Conscience and Prevent a Trump Presidency?," *Rolling Stone*, December 15, 2016, http://www.rollingstone.com/politics/features/will-electors-vote-their-conscience-and-stop-trump-w456167.

[11] Dave Boyer, "Rep. Lewis Says Trump is Not a 'Legitimate' President," *The Washington Times*, January 13, 2017. https://www.washingtontimes.com/news/2017/jan/13/john-lewis-says-trump-not-legitimate-president/.

him from office. So, what should we expect them to do in furtherance of this goal? The answer: Anything and everything.

Do not make the mistake of assuming that the Democrats and the Left will play by traditional rules. They most certainly will not. All political rules and traditions are out the window. No holds are barred. They will try anything and everything, no matter how preposterous or outrageous it may seem to reasonable people. To the Left, this is a war. A war to be won by any means necessary. It is impossible to predict what sleazy tactics or baseless allegations they might dream up. The Left's potential for depravity is without bounds and beyond measure. However, there are some general methods of attack we can anticipate. Let us consider some of them here, so that if and when they are employed, we may recognize them for what they are. As we do so, keep in mind that everything the Left says or does will be in furtherance of their effort to remove President Trump from power, which ultimately must be done through one of the three methods I explained: resignation, the 25th Amendment, or impeachment and conviction.

Outrageous Accusations

The Left will engage in a never-ending witch hunt for anything they can turn into a political scandal. Whether they ever find credible evidence of any type of serious wrongdoing remains to be seen. However, failure to find any will not deter them from claiming that they have. True or not, the allegations of wrongdoing or even criminal behavior will come, and they will come relentlessly. The Left is not constrained by truth or decency. They will make whatever outrageous accusations they think they can get away with politically. Given that the Media is their partner in this effort to destroy Trump, they can and will get away with quite a lot. In fact, you can expect that many, if not most, of the accusations against Trump will come from the Media itself. In many ways, the Media is leading the Democrat Party. While it used to be that Democrat leaders would give marching orders to their allies in the Media, the process now often works in reverse. The Leftist Media oftentimes sets the political strategy and the Democrats march in line behind them. Expect this to continue.

In their ongoing attempt to manufacture political scandals, no accusation will be too outrageous. They will level any and all accusations which can be conjured in their minds. Nothing and no one is off limits. They will attack the President. They will attack anyone in his administration. They will attack anyone from the campaign. They will attack his supporters. They will attack anyone with whom he had business dealings. They will attack his friends. They will attack his family. They will attack his children. They will attack the tailor who altered his pants, if need be. There is no one they will not attack if they believe it will harm Trump in any way. They will destroy careers. They will destroy reputations. They will destroy lives.

Casualties are to be expected in war, and this is war to the Left. If they can damage the President by destroying someone else, then that is exactly what they will do.

As the Left accuses and attacks, they will use language of the most exaggerated and incendiary kind. Everything will be a "scandal." Everything will be "corruption." Everything will be a "crisis." Everything will be a "crime." Everything President Trump says or does will be the worst version of that particular thing which has ever been said or done in American history. Routine actions that other Presidents have taken without criticism will suddenly become constitutional violations of the highest order. The term "constitutional crisis" will be used often. And this will be no accident, for terms such as this raise the specter of impeachment. After all, if the President violates the Constitution in such a way as to cause a "crisis," then impeachment is the obvious remedy.

These accusations will routinely come from anonymous sources, many from inside the Trump Administration itself. It has become obvious to anyone who pays even the slightest attention, that career Leftists inside the Executive Branch view it as their mission to aid the Democrats and the Media in driving Trump from office. To protect their identity, and to further the cause of destroying Trump, journalists will eagerly report whatever these "Deep State" saboteurs tell them. They will not even attempt to verify the accuracy of the information before reporting it, and because the source is anonymous, nobody else will be able to either. Since their sources will be government employees, journalists will identify them as "government officials." This is how false allegations against the President will be concocted and given legitimacy. Deep State leakers can make up virtually any spurious accusations they wish. Unfortunately, whatever is reported by the Media is swallowed hook, line, and sinker by a large percentage of the American People.

Investigations

Along with most of their allegations, will come calls for investigations. So serious will be the Left's accusations against the President, that the American People will be said to "deserve" and "demand" answers! The first step will be calls for investigations by Congressional oversight committees. Since Democrats seem to control Congress, whether they are in the majority or not, you can bet that there will be many committees in both the House and Senate conducting investigations of the Trump Administration. After all, one of the best and most reliable assets of the Left is the cowardice of the Republican Party, who can always be counted on to acquiesce to their demands. During committee hearings, Democrats will use their allotted time to serve up red meat for the crazies that make up the base of their party, and to ingratiate themselves to the Media. Some Congressmen and Senators will surely call on the

President to resign or demand that Congress consider impeachment. In addition, always desperate for approval by the Leftist Media, it would not take much for at least some Republicans to join these calls.

Congressional investigations will not be enough to satisfy the Left, however. As the Legislative Branch, Congress does not possess the authority to prosecute. As long as an investigation is taking place only in Congress, the Democrats cannot believably claim that Trump is under "criminal investigation." Given that the ultimate goal is to remove Trump from office, they are desperate to argue criminality. Therefore, there will be constant calls for the Justice Department to launch a criminal investigation. Then, every time a Democrat or left-wing journalist speaks or writes about Trump or his administration, they can repeatedly point out that they are under "criminal investigation." This will be an important part of the propaganda effort to convince the American People that President Trump has committed crimes. And what do you do when a President commits crimes? You impeach him and remove him from office, of course! (Unless the President is Bill Clinton. Then you just dismiss his serious felonies, for which anyone else would have been sent to prison, as being "just about sex.")

Now, let us suppose that the Justice Department announces, in their vain attempt to satisfy the Left, that they will launch an investigation. Will that satisfy the Left? If you think it will, then I have a big beautiful bridge that I can sell to you for a song. It connects the Magical Kingdom of Purple Unicorns to the Shores of Lollipop Dreams. Wake up! Of course, it won't satisfy the Left! Seriously, have you not been paying attention?

The Left will not settle for a standard investigation. They will insist on an "independent investigation." After all, Trump's Justice Department cannot be trusted to conduct an investigation into Trump himself. Therefore, calls for a "Special Counsel" or, better yet, a "Special Prosecutor" will begin.

The Special Counsel Trap

Calling for a Special Counsel is a trap – a trap into which Republican administrations are tailor-made for falling. Appointing a Special Counsel is almost certainly a mistake, and should be avoided at all cost. Special Counsel appointments offer the allure of removing an investigation from politics – it will do nothing of the kind. Republicans often naively believe that by appointing a Special Counsel they can satisfy the Left and quash the issue until the investigation is complete. It will do neither of these things. First, the Left can never be satisfied. Second, the fact that a Special Counsel is investigating the matter will be used as a rhetorical baseball bat with which to beat the President over the head on a daily basis.

The more important reason that appointing a Special Counsel is almost certainly a mistake, is that it is likely to end poorly for the President, whether he had engaged in wrongdoing or not. Once a Special Counsel is appointed, they are almost untouchable politically, especially if appointed to investigate a Republican President. They have all the resources of the federal government at their disposal and they are answerable to no one. This is dangerous.

What makes a Special Counsel even more dangerous for a President, especially a Republican President, is that their entire purpose is to find a crime – any crime. While their official purpose is ostensibly to "find the truth," the unspoken fact is that without finding a crime with which to accuse the President or some member or members of his administration, the Special Counsel will be forever branded by the Media and the entire Left as a failure, or worse. He might even be accused of engaging in a cover-up of the President's alleged crimes. He would face the very real prospect of having his career and reputation ruined. This creates the perverse incentive for the Special Counsel to find a crime at all cost.

In trying to find a crime, the Special Counsel would not be limited to the underlying issue he was specifically appointed to investigate. The investigative mandate is usually broad enough to include any and all matters and individuals even tangentially connected to the issue. A Special Counsel could expand the scope of his investigation virtually at will. When you consider the thousands of criminal laws we have in this country, and the ambiguous language of many statutes, it is not difficult to find some crime that the President, or someone connected to him, can be accused of having committed. If that means twisting the clear meaning of a criminal statute in order to charge someone with a crime, so be it!

Another problem with Special Counsel Investigations is their potential for official expansion. That an investigation begins with a limited scope and defined purpose, is no guarantee that it will stay within those parameters. Once the Justice Department caves to political pressure and appoints a Special Counsel, it will have opened the flood gates. The Left will constantly push to expand the scope of the investigation. The reason is obvious. The Left's purpose in seeking an investigation is not to find the truth or to pursue justice, it is to find something, anything, to use as grounds for impeachment or, at the very least, to so weaken the President politically that he is unable to advance his agenda. Therefore, the Democrats will insist that every allegation, whether credible or not, be added to the scope of the Special Counsel's investigation. Even better, appoint a new Special Counsel to investigate the new allegations. After all, multiple investigations are better than one!

Any refusal by the Justice Department to increase the scope of the investigation, or to appoint a new Special Counsel, would be described as a "cover-up." Having succumbed to political pressure once, it is likely they would do so again. On and on, this process could continue, seemingly without end. What would begin as a narrowly-targeted investigation, could turn into a perpetual witch hunt.

This is not to suggest that a Special Counsel investigation could not ultimately exonerate a President, it could – theoretically. More likely, however, is that it will not. Even if an investigation turns up no evidence of a crime, the Special Counsel will almost certainly not issue a report in which he declares the President's innocence. He will use language such as "we could not find enough evidence to file charges," or "not enough evidence to prove guilt beyond a reasonable doubt," or some other similar formulation. Hardly an exoneration. Thus, even if the investigation produces no evidence of prosecutable crimes or impeachable offenses, the political damage will have been done. It may be minimal, or it could destroy a Presidency. In any event, it is almost impossible for a President to emerge unscathed and undamaged.

Finally, the appointment of a Special Counsel should be resisted for a more basic, yet exceedingly important reason. In my opinion, Special Counsel Investigations are dangerous and they are fundamentally un-American. The way our justice system is supposed to work is that we investigate crimes and find the people responsible. Special Counsel Investigations turn this process on its head, no matter what their official mandate is purported to be. In reality, they investigate people with the express purpose of finding crimes.

Criminal Prosecution

If the goal is to impeach President Trump and remove him from office, what better way than to charge him with a crime? You don't think that would ever happen? Don't be so sure. Let us examine the question.

Whether a President can be prosecuted while in office is an open constitutional question. There are many viewpoints among constitutional scholars who argue that a sitting President cannot be subjected to a criminal prosecution. One argument is that because prosecution is an Executive Branch function, and since the President is the singular Executive, he cannot prosecute himself. Others cite Article I, Section 3, Clause 7 of the Constitution which states:

> *Judgment in cases of impeachment shall not extend further than to removal from office, and disqualification to hold and enjoy any office of honor, trust or profit under the United States: <u>but the party convicted shall nevertheless be liable and subject to indictment, trial, judgment and punishment, according to law</u>.*
>
> (emphasis added)

They argue that because the Constitution provides that a President may be prosecuted after he has been removed from office through impeachment and conviction, he can therefore only be prosecuted after he leaves office.

For its part, the official policy of the United States Department of Justice, as of this writing, is that a sitting President may not be indicted or criminally prosecuted. The DOJ's position and reasoning were explained in a 1973 memorandum and reaffirmed in 2000.[12] According to their legal analysis, since Article II of the Constitution vests all executive authority in the President alone, indicting him or otherwise subjecting him to criminal prosecution would "impermissibly undermine the capacity of the executive branch to perform its constitutionally assigned functions."

Therefore, it would violate DOJ policy for a federal prosecutor to pursue a criminal prosecution against the President. However, that does not mean it could not happen. If criminal charges were to be filed against the President by a federal prosecutor, whether a Special Counsel, U.S. Attorney, or other DOJ lawyer, it would certainly not be the first time that department policies were ignored in furtherance of political ends. It would, without question, be the most egregious and outrageous violation of DOJ policy in American history, but again, that does not mean it could not happen.

---

[12] U.S. Department of Justice, A Sitting President's Amenability to Indictment and Criminal Prosecution, Memorandum Opinion for the Attorney General, by Randolph D. Moss, October 16, 2000, https://www.justice.gov/sites/default/files/olc/opinions/2000/10/31/op-olc-v024-p0222_0.pdf.

If President Trump were indicted for a crime while in office, there would be a legal battle over the question of whether or not a prosecution could proceed while he is President. The arguments cited above, as well as others, would be argued vigorously from all sides. From a purely theoretical standpoint, the debate would be fascinating. For the politics of our country however, it would be disastrous.

The constitutional issues involved would, to some extent, depend upon the level of government at which charges were brought. Under our Constitution, the federal and state criminal justice systems are completely separate. So, while the President is head of the Executive Branch of the federal government, he holds no authority in the states. Therefore, the argument that he cannot prosecute himself would not apply if charges were brought against him in a state court. However, other constitutional arguments, such as those to which the DOJ policy currently adheres, would be applicable against a state prosecution as well. However, state prosecutors are not bound by DOJ policies, and at least to that extent, would not be prohibited from bringing a prosecution against the President. Whether or not the prosecution would be allowed to proceed, while the President is in office, would ultimately be determined by the courts.

Putting aside the constitutional arguments about whether a prosecution against a sitting President would be allowed to proceed, is there any real chance that Trump would be charged with crime? In this climate out-of-control Leftist hatred and rage, I say yes, there most certainly is that possibility. If Trump were to be indicted, or otherwise charged with a crime, (not all crimes need to be charged by indictment), the politics make it more likely that such charges would be filed in a state court, not a federal court. Let us examine the reasons.

In my opinion, criminal charges are not likely to ever be filed against a sitting President in federal court. First, the constitutional arguments that a President cannot be prosecuted while in office are stronger as applied against federal charges, given the theoretical absurdity of the President prosecuting himself. Second, as I stated, the current policy of the Department of Justice is that a sitting President may not be subjected to criminal prosecution. Thus, it would be a violation of DOJ policy for a federal prosecutor, including any Special Counsel, to bring a criminal prosecution against the President. Finally, if there is evidence to prove that the President committed a crime, there is no need to go through the constitutional legal battle which would ensue. The easier, and better, option would be to simply use the alleged criminal violations as the basis for impeachment proceedings. If the President is removed from office, he can then be prosecuted (assuming he is not pardoned, of course).

It is more likely, if President Trump is to be charged with a crime, that such charges would be filed in a state court. First, some of the constitutional arguments that a President cannot be prosecuted while in office are less strong as applied to state charges. Second, there are many more prosecutors in the states, and not a single one is a political subordinate of the President, as is every federal prosecutor. None of them is employed by, or answerable to, the President of the United States. State prosecutors derive their authority from the states, not the federal government – they are wholly separate.

Third, and most importantly, the reason that criminal charges might be brought in a state court is that a state prosecutor somewhere might possess a strong personal motivation to charge President Trump with a crime. There are plenty of far-left prosecutors around the country. Like most Leftists, many of them are possessed of an irrational hatred for anyone on the Right, and President Trump in particular. For personal political reasons, many would no-doubt love to prosecute Trump. Beyond that however, some may view filing charges against President Trump as a way to fame, fortune, and perhaps a political career of their own. After all, many state prosecutors are themselves elected politicians with visions of grandeur.

Imagine for a moment what would happen if a local District Attorney had President Trump indicted. He would immediately become a national hero to the Left. He would be praised endlessly by the Media. No matter the ultimate outcome, he would be virtually guaranteed a multimillion-dollar book deal. He could get his own show on MSNBC, CNN or any number of other Leftist media outlets. If he lives in a Blue State, he would be the immediate front-runner for any political office he sought. If he lives in a Red State, he can just move to a Blue State and be the front-runner there – New York, for example, is always kind to left-wing carpetbaggers. You see my point. There is enormous opportunity for fame, fortune, and career advancement for any obscure state prosecutor who brings charges against President Trump.

Keep in mind also, that as a billionaire businessman, Donald Trump has had dealings in one form or another in many states across the country. Certainly, an ambitious political-hack Democrat prosecutor somewhere can find some criminal statute sufficiently ambiguous to misapply to some business dealing Trump had in his state. This is what makes using the criminal justice system for political purposes so dangerous. Once a person becomes the target of a politically-motivated prosecutor, all notions of justice and equal application of the law go out the window.

Furthermore, filing criminal charges against a person is oftentimes not difficult, especially for a prosecutor unburdened by ethics or fidelity to the law. Many state crimes, even those which carry the possibility of significant jail time, can be charged simply by a prosecutor filing paperwork. More serious crimes, felonies, usually require either a finding of probable cause by a judge at a preliminary hearing or a true bill of indictment by a grand jury.

You likely have heard it said that a good prosecutor could indict a ham sandwich. This speaks to how easy it is for a prosecutor to get a grand jury to indict someone. Grand juries meet in secret under the direction of a prosecutor. They usually consider only that evidence which is presented to them by the prosecutor or under his direction. Mitigating evidence is seldom presented. There are no rules of evidence. Hearsay, which would be largely inadmissible at trial, is routinely presented. There is no cross-examination of witnesses. Neither the accused nor his counsel has a right to be present or to be heard. In short, the grand jurors see what the prosecutor wants them to see, and nothing that he doesn't. If, on the rare occasion that a grand jury does not indict a person as the prosecutor wishes, he can simply convene a new grand jury and seek an indictment from them. The Constitution's prohibition against double jeopardy[13] does not apply to grand jury proceedings. Oftentimes, as you can see, a grand jury is little more than a rubber stamp for the prosecutor.

If it ever comes to pass that state criminal charges are filed against President Trump, they would almost certainly trigger impeachment hearings in the House of Representatives. Congress would not wait for the legal battle, which could drag on for years, to be resolved. The filing of criminal charges alone

---

[13] U.S. Constitution, 5th Amendment

would lend credibility to the allegations. Therefore, it wouldn't matter how the state criminal charges are ultimately resolved. They could even be dropped or thrown out of court, and it wouldn't matter. They would have served their purpose.

PART III The Consequences for America

The Left's obsessive hatred of President Donald Trump, and their crusade to remove him from power by any means necessary, has the potential to cause serious long-term damage to the country. What we are witnessing is not normal political opposition. The Left has moved far beyond that.

Undermining the President's Legitimacy

Let us be clear. Politically opposing a President of the United States, even vehemently so, is perfectly legitimate. Using the checks and balances of our constitutional system to frustrate his intentions and prevent him from enacting his agenda is also well within the bounds of legitimate political opposition. After all, the President is not a king. The Framers of our Constitution created a system that makes it difficult for elected officials, including the President, to take action without broad political consensus. This was intentional.

Let us also be clear about what is not legitimate. Refusing to accept the will of the People as expressed in a democratic election is not legitimate. Attempting to destroy a presidency by deceiving the American People with non-stop lies and baseless allegations of criminal wrongdoing and constitutional violations is not legitimate. Using the constitutional process of impeachment, designed as a remedy for criminal or deleterious actions of a president, in order to remove a man from office simply because you could not defeat him in an open and fair election, is most certainly not legitimate. Indeed, much of the Left's opposition to President Trump is a far cry from legitimate political resistance. It is something different. It is an effort to destroy a President for no reason other than that he won the election.

One of the ways in which they have endeavored to destroy the Trump Presidency, is by calling into question the integrity of the 2016 election itself. Having failed to defeat him with votes, they now seek to de-legitimize him as President. The best example of this effort thus far is the allegation that a foreign power engineered the outcome of our election.

Since long before President Trump was inaugurated, we have been treated to non-stop allegations that Russia "hacked" the election.[14] That not a single Democrat can tell you what Russia supposedly did to swing the election in Trump's favor is irrelevant. The ambiguous allegation is designed to undermine the legitimacy of his election, and that is all that matters. They want Americans to believe that their President was not rightfully elected. That he is exercising constitutional authority not granted to him by the People. This is dangerous.

---

[14] Brian Bennett and W.J. Hennigan, "Obama orders full review of Russian hacking during the 2016 election," *Los Angeles Times*, December 9, 2017, http://www.latimes.com/nation/la-na-hacking-election-20161209-story.html.

In our Republic, the peaceful transition of power, and the peaceful governance by those whom we elect, requires the faith of the American People that our elections are open and fair, and that their outcomes are lawful and legitimate. What the Left is doing runs counter to the ideals of representative democracy and undermines the proper functioning of our constitutional republic.

To create the belief in the American People, through a campaign of lies, that our elections are not fair and that our elected leaders are exercising power not legitimately conferred upon them is to undermine confidence in the system itself. This is dangerous. In the short-term, it can lead to civil unrest and violence as those who feel cheated and betrayed seek retribution. In the long-term, the effects can be even more profound and destructive. Once the belief sets in among the People that our institutions and constitutional processes are corrupt and fraudulent, they lose their perceived legitimacy. At that point, anarchy may begin to take hold as they rebel against a system believed to be unjust. Once we start down that road, where it leads is anyone's guess.

The Dangers of a Paralyzed Presidency

Believe it or not, it is actually important that we have a President. It may come as a surprise to those on the Left, many of whom are wholly unfamiliar with Article II of the

Constitution (or even basic civics for that matter), but the duties and obligations of the President of the United States are substantial.

All executive authority is vested in the President. That means that it is his responsibility to take care that the laws of our country are faithfully executed. In addition to that, he has primary authority over foreign policy and is Commander-in-Chief of the military. In short, the President is responsible for national security and the safety of the American People. Given the dangerous world in which we live, this is serious stuff. It is imperative that we have a President who can effectively do his job. Nothing less than the lives and the future of the American People may depend upon it.

This is yet another reason why what the Left is doing is so dangerous and irresponsible. It is dangerous for our country to have a President whose time is consumed by defending himself against constant attacks meant to destroy his Presidency and to drive him from office. We need a President who can focus on doing his job rather than trying to keep his job. Investigating a President, or even attempting to impeach and remove him from office, for real and serious allegations of wrongdoing, is one thing. Indeed, doing so under such circumstances may very well be the right thing to do. However, relentless attempts to drive him from office for purely political reasons is something quite different.

Furthering the Divide

America is a country deeply divided. At few times in history, have our political and cultural divisions ever run so deep. Our regional divisions are obvious. Generally speaking, it is North versus South and the coasts versus the interior of the country. More accurately, the regional divide exists between large urban areas and everywhere else. The people in these respective areas live vastly different lives. Their values are different. Their lifestyles are different. Their politics are virtually incompatible. In many ways, it is as if they are living in completely different societies. The undeniable truth is that things are only getting worse.

Advances in communication technology have helped to exacerbate and accelerate our divisions. We now segregate ourselves by the news and information we consume. No longer stuck with the same few corporate media outlets, we can now get our news from a seemingly infinite number of sources. This has led to our current situation in which many people seek out only information and opinion which reinforces their worldview. More and more, based upon the way we get our news, Americans on the Left and Right cannot even agree on a basic set of facts with respect to almost any issue facing our country. We are increasingly unable to get along because we cannot even have a discussion proceeding from a common understanding of the world. Recently, we have begun to see an increased number of incidents in which our political divisions have led to violence. It seems as if our body politic is sitting precariously upon a powder keg. It needs only the right spark to explode.

Given this context, the Left's obsession to destroy President Trump is particularly perilous. First, the hyperbolic language and argumentation used by the Left has no effect other than to inflame tensions and further divide people. They offer no legitimate policy-based criticisms of President Trump. Every criticism is simply a personal attack upon his character. Everything he does or says is, according to the Left, the result of his racism, sexism, homophobia, religious bigotry or some other manifestation of hatred or prejudice. The problem with this approach, other than it being patently ridiculous, is that such allegations against Trump are implicitly allegations against his supporters – and his supporters know it.

Every time the Left accuses President Trump of being a racist (or sexist, homophobe, bigot, etc) for holding a certain policy position, they are effectively calling everyone who agrees with that position a racist as well. This tactic does absolutely nothing except anger and alienate Trump supporters even further. Calling people racists, or some other personal slur, does not persuade those people to your position. It only makes them despise you. Furthermore, by constantly accusing Trump supporters of being hateful bigots, the Left convinces themselves that it is true. This only serves to feed their own anger and hatred. With their irrational Trump loathing, the Left is pushing us further and further into a self-reinforcing loop of personal hostility.

This injection of concentrated animus into our politics will have repercussions which will far outlive the Trump Presidency. Donald Trump will not be President forever. What lasting damage will the Left's hatred for President Trump have caused? Hatred is not easily wiped away. It lingers. It often festers and grows more intense. It will not leave us once Trump is out of office. Make no mistake, the Left's obsessive hatred for Trump will have a lasting effect on us all.

Denying the Will of the People

As stated in the Declaration of Independence, a fundamental principle upon which our republic was founded is that the government derives its "just powers from the consent of the governed." The government has no authority except that which we confer upon it. In delegating specifically enumerated powers to each branch of government, the Constitution defines the scope of the authority we confer. We choose specific people to exercise this authority on our behalf through our elections. It is in this way that we give our consent.

We, the People, have a right that those whom we have specifically chosen to govern in our names, be allowed to do so. Unjustly removing a duly-elected President from office, or preventing him from exercising his authority, is to deny We, the

People, our right to self-governance. Unless extraordinary circumstances amounting to "treason, bribery, or other high crimes and misdemeanors" warrant the President's removal from office, any effort to do so is an assault upon the People.

In 2016, the American People clearly expressed their will in electing Donald Trump as President. After enduring eight years of far-left governance by the Obama Administration, the country chose a new course. We clearly rejected the candidate who would have continued Obama's policies in favor of one who offered a radical change in direction. The difference between the candidates was stark, making the will of the People all the easier to discern. States that had not voted for a Republican candidate for President in a generation did so in this election. The People spoke, and we spoke clearly.

Having chosen Donald Trump as our President, it is our right to have him exercise the authority that the Constitution grants to his office. For the Left to remove him, by impeachment or otherwise, for no reason other than pure partisan politics, would be to reject the will of the People.

To this proposition, the Left would no-doubt offer the following rebuttal (to the extent that they could cobble together an intelligible response at all):

> "Would it not also be the will of the People if their elected representatives in Congress were to impeach the President and remove him from office?"

Ah, excellent question! The answer is a definite maybe. (No, this is not the lawyer in me speaking. I am serious.) In this book, I have discussed the fact that the Left is obsessed with destroying President Trump and removing him from office by any means necessary, and for whatever reason – legitimate or not. If, for example, they successfully remove Trump from office through the impeachment process, for reasons that do not amount to "high crimes and misdemeanors," then no, this cannot rightly be said to be the will of the People.

Under our constitutional system, the will of the People extends only to their elected representatives exercising authority duly granted to them by the Constitution. With respect to the power of impeachment, the Constitution extends this authority to the House of Representatives only for actions that amount to "treason, bribery, or other high crimes and misdemeanors." To impeach a President and remove him from office for alleged actions that do not meet this standard, cannot rightly be said to be the will of the People. It is, in fact, a rejection of it.

As I have discussed, impeachment is a political process, not a legal one. Congress determines what constitutes "high crimes and misdemeanors." In truth, with the requisite number of votes, they can impeach President Trump and remove him from office for whatever reason they choose. Perhaps they will decide that mocking Rosie O'Donnell is an impeachable offense!

That aside, Congress would be wise to consider impeachment only for serious cases in which it is actually warranted. If President Trump does commit acts which amount to "treason, bribery, or other high crimes and misdemeanors" then he absolutely should be impeached and removed from office. We should not tolerate such conduct from any President. In my opinion, we have not used the impeachment clause enough in our history. Many Presidents should have been removed from office for their conduct, but they were protected by partisan politics. With respect to President Trump, however, he has done absolutely nothing to this point to warrant even a serious discussion about impeachment. Of course, facts do not matter to the Left, which leads us to the potential danger.

With their irresponsible and hysterical talk about impeaching President Trump, they have created a two-fold problem for the country. First, by calling for his impeachment non-stop since before he even took office, the Left has created the potential for a "Boy Who Cried Wolf" scenario. Most people who are not of the Left have tuned them out and do not take them seriously on this issue. So much so that if Trump were to commit an impeachable offense, many people who might otherwise have taken the allegations seriously may not do so because they have heard the Left demanding impeachment for so long and for obviously disingenuous reasons. If everything he does is an "impeachable offense," then to many people, nothing is an "impeachable offense."

Second, the Left has so convinced themselves that President Trump should be impeached, that if the Democrats regain control of Congress, they will almost certainly attempt to do so for whatever reason, no matter how trivial or contrived. This could be disastrous. To put the country through the ordeal of impeachment on the basis of baseless allegations, or those that do not rise to the constitutional standard of an impeachable offense, could precipitate civil unrest, violence, and political chaos the likes of which most of us have not seen in our lifetimes — perhaps not since the Civil War. This is not hyperbole. This is not a game. These are potential real-world consequences.

Final Admonition

The modern American Left is a loose conglomeration of disparate groups motivated by the worst aspects of human nature. More than any other characteristic, it is their hatred which gives them common purpose and leads them to action. Hatred cannot be appealed to with reason. There is no compromise with those motivated by hate. There is no getting along. The only responsible way to deal with hatred is to oppose it and defeat it, lest it infect the entire system and destroy us all.

The Left's primary opposition to President Trump is hatred alone. The evidence for this is their own words and actions. With their words, they offer nothing but personal insults of the most vicious and baseless kind. What they do not offer is a coherent explanation of legitimate political differences. With their actions, they increasingly resort to violence. From Inauguration Day forward, the Left has engaged in rioting as a means of expressing their hatred disguised as political dissent. Simply seeing a fellow American wearing a red "Make America Great Again" hat is reason enough for Leftists to turn violent.[15] A scheduled speech by a pro-Trump author is

---

[15] Chris White, "VIDEO: Trump Staffer Allegedly Assaulted for Wearing 'Make America Great Again' Hat on College Campus," Law & Crime, November 7, 2016, https://lawandcrime.com/video/video-trump-staffer-allegedly-assaulted-for-wearing-make-america-great-again-hat-on-college-campus/.

Stephanie Ramirez, "Student Attacked for Waring 'Make America Great Again Hat' at Anti-Trump Protest," WUSA9.com, November 16, 2016, http://www.wusa9.com/news/local/maryland/student-attacked-for-wearing-trump-hat-at-anti-trump-protest-parent-says/352788338.

Paul Elias, "Student wearing Trump hat beaten at UC Berkeley after protest," The Boston Globe, February 2, 2017, https://www.bostonglobe.com/news/nation/2017/02/02/student-wearing-trump-hat-beaten-berkeley-after-protest/htFyg9NRPl0Q5BQI7zhNyH/story.html.

Matt Sczesny, "Middle School Student Attacked on Bus for Wearing 'Make America Great Again' Hat," WKMOV.com, February 6, 2017, http://www.kmov.com/story/34424524/middle-school-student-attacked-on-bus-for-wearing-make-america-great-again-hat.

all it takes for them to form violent mobs and assault people, smash windows, loot stores and set fire to cars.[16]

The Left suffers from a sickness of hatred and rage. It did not spring up spontaneously in response to the election of President Trump. It has been growing and intensifying for decades. It was given a sense of legitimacy and entitlement during the eight years of the Obama Presidency. Having unexpectedly lost their hold on political power, the Left now focuses all their energy on destroying the one person they view as responsible for their loss. Trump is not the reason for their hatred, he is the target of it. Those who are motivated by hate must have an enemy to destroy, and so they must destroy Trump.

The great danger comes from the fact that these people are no longer just a fringe minority. While they once made up only a small part of the Democrat Party, they now control it. Though many of his accomplishments are being wiped away, owing largely to the fact that he did so much by executive order alone, Barack Obama's lasting legacy may be the final transformation of the Democrats into a far-left, radicalized party of hatred and intolerance.

---

[16] James Doubek, "Breitbart Editor's Event Canceled As Protests Turn Violent At UC Berkeley," *National Public Radio*, February 2, 2017, https://www.npr.org/sections/thetwo-way/2017/02/02/512992000/breitbart-editors-event-canceled-as-protests-turn-violent-at-uc-berkeley.

If the Left has its way, President Trump will be impeached and removed from office. Doing so for legitimate reasons would be one thing. Doing so without just cause, motivated by nothing but obsessive hatred is quite another. Were this ever to happen, it would be a dark day for America. It would mark a turning point in our history. We would cease to be the republic we have been, in which elections are respected as the will of the People. We would have transformed into a society in which political tribalism is all that matters. A society in which any means are legitimate so long as the right ends are achieved.

In our republic, process is important. Under our Constitution, the processes and limits on government protect and ensure our inalienable rights. In our courts of law, it is the process which protects and ensures our legal rights. In our politics, it is the process which gives legitimacy to the outcome of elections. Without respect for, and faith in our processes, we could easily descend into chaos and anarchy. So balkanized has our society become, and so divisive our politics, that it would not take much. With so little that unites us anymore, were we to lose faith in our constitutional processes, the results could be calamitous. In the end, the Left's obsession to take down President Trump at all cost is far more than just a threat to his presidency, it is a very real threat to our republic.

29709018R00044

Made in the USA
Lexington, KY
02 February 2019